C is for CHRISTMAS

MICHELLE MEDLOCK ADAMS

Illustrated by Louise Hargreaves

little lamb
BOOKS

C is for Christmas

Text copyright © 2018 Michelle Medlock Adams

Illustrations copyright © 2018 Louise Hargreaves

ISBN-Hardcover: 978-1-7323158-0-8
ISBN-Softcover: 978-1-7323158-9-1
ISBN-EBook: 978-1-7323158-8-4
LCCN: 2018945401

Little lamb
BOOKS

Published by Little Lamb Books
www.littlelambbooks.com
P.O. Box 211724, Bedford, TX 76095

Design by TLC Book Design, TLCBookDesign.com

First Edition
Printed and bound in Canada

For Ang:
You were my very first friend,
and you're my forever friend.
Love Ya!
– Miss

A *is for* ANGELS

The ANGELS came to praise the Lord.
They all began to sing:
"Glory to God in the highest."
It was an awesome thing.

Christmas is the Lord's BIRTHDAY.
We celebrate his birth!
God gave his greatest gift to us.
When Jesus came to earth.

Happy Birtday Jesus

icing sugar

Jam

grannys recipies

B *is for*
BIRTHDAY

C *is for*
CHRISTMAS

CHRISTMAS comes
just once a year.
It is a special season.

Santa Claus
is really great,
but Jesus is the reason!

DECEMBER
is quite magical.
The best month
of the year.
We decorate
and celebrate
and spread the
Christmas cheer!

D *is for* **DECEMBER**

Jesus Christ was born on EARTH
on that first Christmas day.
God sent his son to share his love
and take our sins away.

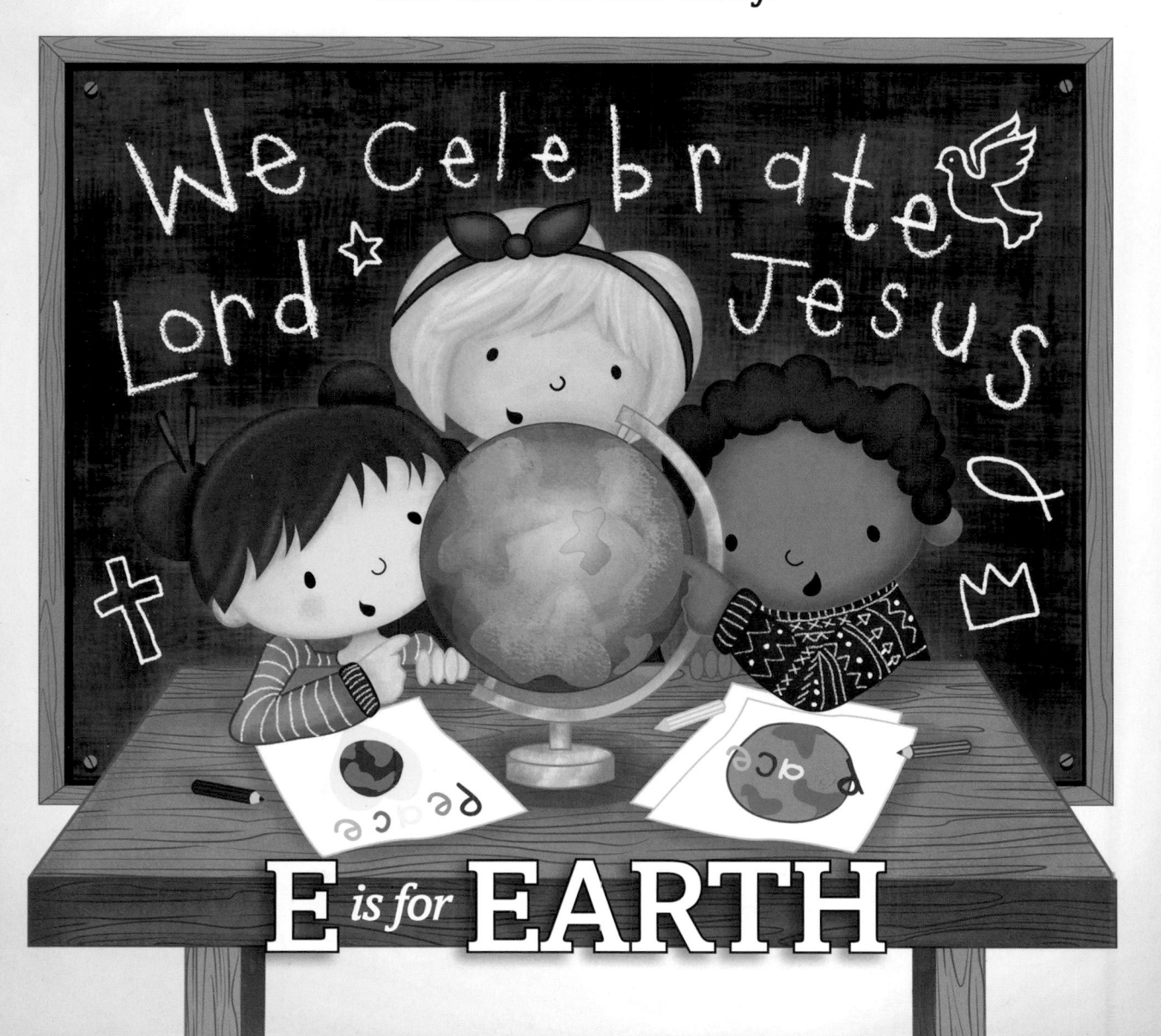

E *is for* EARTH

F is for FAMILY

At Christmas, we make memories
with friends and FAMILY.
Like stringing popcorn on a thread
to decorate the tree.

We sing about
GOODWILL toward men.
It's in a Christmas song.
But we should share
GOODWILL toward men,
right now
and all year long.

G *is for* GOODWILL

H _is for_ HAY

"And this shall be a sign to you,"
the angel boldly said.
"You'll find the babe in
swaddling clothes
upon a small HAY bed."

I *is for* INN

When Mary and Joseph
came to town
the INN was all sold out!
They had to stay inside a barn.
That's strange without a doubt!

When JOSEPH
finally saw the child,
his heart was filled with joy.
He said,
"Jesus will be his name."
He's Daddy's special boy.

J *is for* JOSEPH

K is for KINGS

A babe was born in Bethlehem.
The news spread everywhere.
Three KINGS came from the Orient
to worship Jesus there.

L is for
LIGHTS

At Christmas, we use lots of LIGHTS
to decorate the tree.
We also place LIGHTS on our house
for all the world to see.

The sheep, the goats, the cows, and mice…
All huddled in real tight.
The MANGER was the place to be
on that first Christmas night.

M is for MANGER

The shepherds heard of Jesus' birth
and shared the NEWS abroad.
They said, "We saw the King of Kings!
We saw the Son of God!"

N is for NEWS

We make new ORNAMENTS each year.
We hang them up real high.
That way our cat can't knock them down...
But goodness knows she'll try.

O is for ORNAMENTS

TOYS

At Christmas,
we send PACKAGES
to all our special friends.
But, Jesus is
the greatest gift,
the gift that never ends.

P is for PACKAGES

Q is for QUIET

All is QUIET on Christmas Eve,
once everyone's in bed.
We try to stay awake and see
that jolly man in red.

for
santa and
the reindeers
xx

We tie RIBBONS on packages. We tie them in our hair.
At Christmastime we decorate
with RIBBONS everywhere!

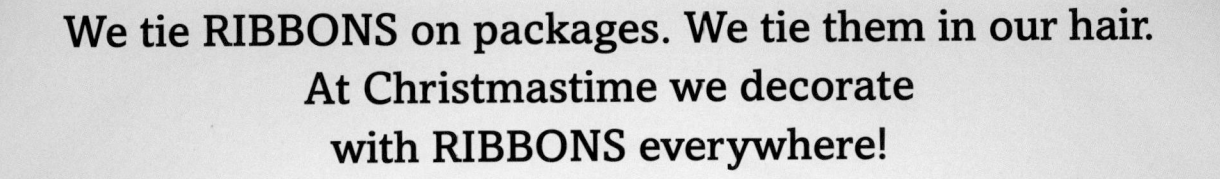

R *is for* RIBBONS

Though it's not always possible,
white Christmases are grand.
The SNOW makes all things beautiful...
A winter wonderland.

S is for SNOW

Each year at Christmas, we bake TREATS.
We spread icing on top.
We eat them one right after one.
They're so good, we can't stop!

T is for TREATS

After we wrap the Christmas gifts,
they go UNDER the tree.
But Puppy likes to lie there, too.
Mom says, "Just let him be."

U *is for* UNDER

Each Christmas,
we pile in the car
to VISIT family.
We drive from house
to house to house…
So many folks to see.

V is for VISIT

W is for WRAPPED

They WRAPPED the babe in swaddling clothes,
and tucked him in real tight.
The King of Kings had come to earth—It was a special night.

X is for XMAS

Though many people think it's fine, XMAS is not the same.
But when we put Christ in Christmas, we magnify his name.

Y *is for* YULETIDE

We have a
YULETIDE festival
at Christmastime
each year.
Our town serves
Wassail—
It's quite nice.
Folks come from
far and near.

When Christmas Day comes to an end
with lots of memories.
We snuggle close in fuzzy robes.
It's time to catch some ZZZZZS.

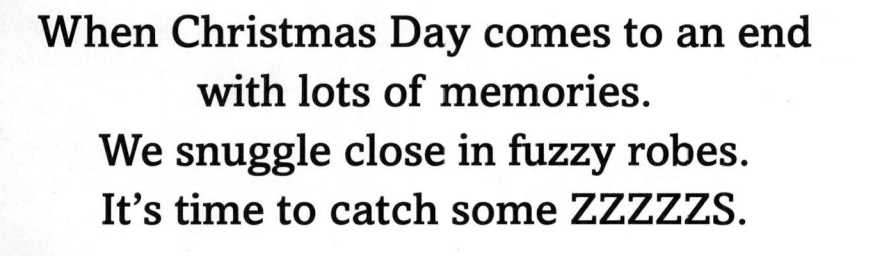

Z is for
ZZZZZS

About the Author

Award-winning and bestselling author MICHELLE MEDLOCK ADAMS loves Christmas music even in October and embraces the true meaning of Christmas as well as the holiday traditions she and her husband, Jeff, have made for their family over the last 27 years. Author of over 80 books, Michelle has won more than 25 writing awards, including four SELAH awards, and is the president of Platinum Literary Services, a premier full-service literary firm. She is a sought after speaker, respected teacher, and a genuine encourager who loves bass fishing and being GiGi to grandson Bear.

You can learn more about Michelle
at www.michellemedlockadams.com.

About the Illustrator

LOUISE HARGREAVES is an illustrator from England. After graduating from Liverpool Art School, Louise worked in the greetings card industry before making the leap to become a freelance designer. She loves to travel, and lived and worked in Australia for a number of years. She eventually returned to her home town to be closer to family, and now lives in a little village in Yorkshire with her husband and 5-year-old daughter Lucy. She loves drawing and painting, being out and about in the countryside, and spending time with her family.

You can learn more about Louise
at www.thebrightagency.com.